# CALL ME BY MY OTHER NAME

## VALERIE WETLAUFER

SIBLING RIVALRY PRESS
LITTLE ROCK, ARKANSAS
DISTURB / ENRAPTURE

Sibling Rivalry Press, LLC
PO Box 26147
Little Rock, AR 72221

info@siblingrivalrypress.com

www.siblingrivalrypress.com

ISBN: 978-1-943977-04-8

Library of Congress Control No: 2015960259

This title is housed permanently in the Rare Books and Special
Collections Vault of the Library of Congress.

First Sibling Rivalry Press Edition, March 2016

# CALL ME BY MY OTHER NAME

*Anna Morris, alias Frank Blunt, the woman who has tried to be a man for the last 15 years was sentenced to the penitentiary for one year. ... She was arrested several months ago in Milwaukee, charged with stealing $175. ... It was then discovered that the prisoner was a woman, although she had worn masculine attire nearly all her life. ... After the sentence had been passed, Gertrude Field, a woman who claimed to have married the prisoner in Eau Claire, fell upon the neck of the prisoner and wept for half an hour.*

—*Badger State Banner*, 1894

*Who are you? and what are you secretly guilty of all your life?*

—Walt Whitman

# MAKE YOU FEEL MY LOVE

*If I could return, it would be with a quiet swagger.*
*Old-fashioned, a little crazy, but sturdy to a fault.*

*I'd follow only paved roads, long for the forest,*
*and swallow love's peril. I'd forgive the way*
*you pick at your fingernails until they bleed.*

*The soapy smell of you would be enough; that tender part*
*on the crown of your head; the verse tattooed at your nape:*
*those curling words spelling, "this one you cannot take from me."*

*Maybe when I return, we won't require authorization.*
*We will become impervious to the glares and ghosts,*
*the toothy politicians who sneer our names*
*like a diagnosis. We won't need taxidermy or lures.*

*Travel will be breezy and slow; we'll share a suitcase.*
*I won't yell so much, and you won't drop the eggs.*

*Once you tucked in your chin and kissed my neck*
*until it bled. The winds were rough, the sea close,*
*the tang of iodine. So many states are afraid of recognition.*

*We huddled in the sand, planned our escape.*
*No election, no fire, no brother could foresee*
*the worst happening. (No hospital. No identification.)*

*Lead paint licked from the radiator. Mold rotted*
*the wooden staircase. Always something more*
*they want concealed. The tarot said Six of Swords,*

*so we knew we had to skedaddle. We crossed a river,*
*fled to a foreign country for our wedding.*
*All your lovers folded napkins neatly, bid farewell.*

*Still, we pay separate taxes and no small measure of shame.*
*When I return, brick and mortar. Knitted booties,*
*quilts. Flags in the front yard and sharpened pencils.*

*Appliances, bone china, a honeymoon. I'll come at once.*
*I'll come at a run, with snacks. I'll put my hands*
*between your legs and catch the slippery child emerging.*

*When I return, there will be no need for maleficence,*
*just our ringed hands, holding.*

## The One with Violets in Her Lap

The fortune teller at the carnival told me
    I would die by fire and deserve it;
    also, love a girl with violets in her lap.

    Her cracking copper fingers traced lines
on my palm, skimmed scars, peered closer;
clicking her tongue, she indicated the star
    at the base of my thumb—crisis.

I think of your tender perennial, the perfume
at your apex that urges, *please, let me love you.*

    Behind me, the fringe of the velvet curtain
    blew in the acrid breeze, separating
the old woman from the noise of the carnival beyond.
*I am prone to accidents*, she said, digging her dirtied
    nail into the crossroads at the line for health.

When you promise to leave, which one
of us are you protecting?

No umber fear, nor ash or flame. I stack the wood
like a shelter to warm us, extinguish wicks
with the tips of my fingers, taunting kismet;
let it come and take me—

## Helpmate I

Barefoot by a stream in white dresses,
my sister & I dropped petals into the river.

She said the current crafted a pattern—
the letter of a husband's name.

I wished for the bookish woman with wild hair,
who smiled for the camera.

The girl from the next farm over
whispers stiff beneath her petticoats.

They say she tamed snakes
beneath her skirts.

## I Have Reached the Hills;
### The Mountains Lie Beyond

I never told a bead nor sheared a lamb,
but when Pa forced me to the barn,

I milked the goats for hours.
We buried both sisters at home,

Ma at rest in the pasture already.
I picked thistle flowers for the graves.

Now I must tend to swollen udders,
painful bleating in my ears.

Ivan Froth asked my hand.
A feedman from Willowsaw,

oats and bits of hay collect in his pant cuffs.
He always finds something to do with his eyes.

Three years older, he drinks twice as much;
I feel the whiskey on my neck.

I, too, know fire and threat.
I'll quit my Master, slit a dozen throats.

The river flows south from here,
and I alone will build a boat.

# First Theft

I wanted some sign for you,
my claim; some bit of silver
stuck to your finger.
A Real Wife needs a ring.
But I spent all our cash
on that stale cake in Merrimac.
Sugar for my sugar.

The ring I caught was far too big,
but you squealed, wound a blue
thread along its underside
to hold my promise fast,
your appetite whetted.

Baby booties; embroidery
practiced for school. Fashion plates
& catalogs, baubles & habiliments.
Still a girl & all your dreams ready
for the trunk—your hope chest,
eager to be filled.

I have seen my shadow;
there is no end.

*All girls should be nicer.          Conjure these familiars.*

*Gertrude's tender caresses.*

*How fetching Anna*

*must have looked in a cap and pants.*

*Vice and beauty have been my weaknesses, also.*

## Epidemic: Diphtheria

Today I missed you so much I thought I'd follow you.
This town is bare after the fires and funerals.

Mama wouldn't have noticed me going.
She spends all day tending chickens,

hands searching for something in the warmth beneath them,
fingers braiding empty air where Emily's hair should be.

*

Mama went to Church and took the cup.
Emily and Sarah were baptized,

breaking bread—flies and fainting.
Emily succumbed, gasping for vacant air.

Every stitch of clothing had to be burned.
Mama's red knit scarf, chemises, pantalettes,

corsets and aprons, bustles and bonnets.
Even the Sunday clothes and fine silk gowns

Mama wore to visit her kin in the City.
Muslin burns brightest.

*

I made it as far as the road to Winona,
but the weather turned. I thought of the livestock

in the fields, the cows who kept our secrets.
When I am gone, no one will bring them to the barn.

Papa cleans his shotgun idly and searches the skies.
I pass the dark dreaming of every wish fulfilled—

cream, butter-yellow, lavender and black—
Valencienne, Chantilly, and Spanish laces.

All the catalogs instruct:
Vanity is the duty of a proper wife.

The new issue came while you roamed
for work. I folded the corner of so many pages—

the latest styles: spring shirt waists, cashmere cloaks.
When we wed, I will be a perfect replica,

a fashion plate, draped in grosgrain silk
at any price; no one will question our probity.

And what do *you* do in the dark?
Is there someone making sure you're warm,

someone to corral you as the sun slips back into snow
and night's noises bewitch?

Gone: more than half the infants in town—
the immigrants on far farms.

We stripped the woods for coffin lumber,
loosened soil on the banks from all our digging.

Even the girls were sent away to school.
Teacher crying on the train,

her brother Tommy the first one buried.
She held me tight and wept into my hair.

I felt her touch, a burn beneath my slip,
though her hands stayed firm on my back.

At night I count bodies in my brain, so many coffins
and dried blooms, but my kin had no Foxgloves or Prairie Asters,

petals they loved to collect in the summer,
from fields strewn with flowers not tombs.

They say the snow kills this bug, but inside wheezing
persists. They've closed the library for good now.

I keep your knife beneath my dress. My thighs keep
the metal warm. Its sheathed blade brushes my skin as I run.

## Vigilante Committee

Outlaws are overrunning Grant County.
Farmers formed a vigilance committee.
*Fever licks us & drought parches crops.*

Knocking at each loose barn door, looking for women
or drugs, a tramp to chase & burn to the edge of town.

I buy a new belt & cinch my trousers tight,
but when old Farmer Hull shot himself with a revolver
in the harness shop, same sure folks waxed sympathetic:

*It is singular that he should thus take his own life,*
*but I presume it is best that we not look upon him harshly.*

Real men are immune, but I'm inflicted with "Female
Weakness" & will not be left alone.

The town bought a new hearse from Chicago
to cart all the bodies away. Some ladies cut their necks
with sheep shears, throats blooming with blood necklaces.

Raiding sheep & stealing horses won't make me a man,
as much as holding your thighs near mine.

# Helpmate II

Sister posed atop Bessie, the rib-strong mare,
hooves eager, tail twitching;

promised she'd plead Pa's missing clothes
victims of a petty thief.

At school, I stood a head taller, sullen,
refusing to shake my tambourine.

They yanked my neighbor off the track just in time:
she wanted to die because of the gossip.

In the city library, we clutched knees,
gazed at men whose mustaches came loose.

I struggled into trousers,
leather cock cool against my thigh.

Gertrude dubbed me Frank Blunt, unleashed
my hair with a knife, taught me to snitch.

Her warm hand slipped in my pocket; I grew
accustomed to weight resting there.

## NAMING SPELL

Born *Anna* in the fields
under the sun, born goat-tender,
sister-keeper, son-in-a-dress.

*Your name by lightning,*
*your name by whipstitch,*
*your name by the edge of the river,*
*flooding the graves.*

In this town, children slip away so fast.
Grime under our nails sticks despite the lye.
We've been digging graves. We've been pressing
dirty palms together, aiming vain eyes skyward.

*Give everyone a new name.*

Trouser-stealer, field-plower,
straight-talker—*Frank*—without
hair to braid, skirts to lift.
Handsome mustache-wearer.

*Your name by damselfly,*
*your name by thunder,*
*your name at the edge of the river,*
*flooding the graves.*

Funerals more frequent than church.
Boys suicide over sullen women,

sick children buried shallow, suffocating on dirt.
This town is too full from fire.

Smoke stains dresses;
no one weds in white.
What does it matter how close
we stand in the kitchen?

When winds change and the cold comes too strong
for summer, bury your rings behind the barn.

*Your name by cat's claw,*
*your name by terryweather.*
*Your name must change*
*at the edge of this town.*

# Unlike Lesser Gods, I Need No Disguises to Woo

I have fucked all your women,
lain in that bed of rashes with your wives,
your sisters, even a spry mother-in-law.

The youngest ones bathed my upper lip,
while the sullen maternals insisted on feeding me.
They lined up by my tent flap with their offerings,

& some requested to sleep beside me, their tiny backs
pressed against my knees, a cascade of tangled girls
on Egyptian cotton that never caught a stain.

Yet one by one, they rose from me, traipsing back
to their brothers, their husbands, resentfully
bearing lists of chores & children & errands to run.

I have fucked all your women & sent them home,
dresses wilting & smelling of my palms,

dark-eyed girls with feisty teeth & sweat.
Each woman whispered a wish upon departing,
a request they feared I would grant.

These wishes are for you—for thick broth
& wings, sons & softer deaths. No need
for them to make appeals.

Of them I know what is wanted.

*Concerning dreams,*

There are at least two kinds: cultivated & unconscious; sometimes you deserve to be tied down; it is beyond your control; there are the selfish, the materialistic, the sexual;

> *if my own mind can play tricks, how to guard against what comes at us from outside;*

if your brain conjures the unpalatable, that reveals a secret; if you crave things both toothsome & twee; everything is metaphor;

> *is there a way to translate her into a man as fearsome in waking life as dreams;*

if you want to go anywhere with her, you must immerse yourself fully, until you can't tear apart; dress so as not to tell one from the other; sew her to your side so she shall not stray; this happens best in dreams clouded with smoke, men's shoes and birds; anything foreshadowing;

> *I walked into a room of nakedness, a roomful of white; there were words on the walls and the corner shadows deep; dogs hid there and growled, though I could not see them, and I knew that the dogs were what I wanted but wouldn't let myself have;*

Nightmares are traps chosen because you want to be undone; the next night comes even closer; there are things you must consider, such as transience and temperature; dream of clean lines with integrity on dresses and pages and a disembodied voice that tells you when to shut the door.

*Your body appeared clearest, my name emblazoned in shadow on your skin, pert and gleaming, as though you'd never said fear or feather; at your side was a rope, beginning to uncoil;*

## So Long as Men-Folk Stay Away

I know your weakness for sturdy-breasted lace.
My ribs don't bend easy, but when I met you,

I strung my corset tight. With such diminutive hands,
my waist need be small if you're to encircle it.

I remember the first night, when you took off
your spectacles and your eyes shook liquor into me.

I had a bed—big enough and good enough to take you in.
You tasted like almonds, like poison.

I understand you having to leave.
No money to be had in Black River Falls.

So off you go, trying to pass testing yourself
in the bed of every town whore.

Do you long for the scolding and pinched ears
and all you know awaits you?

I've never been Hell on wheels,
but I can live in true outlaw style.

We'll disguise ourselves as raw-boned
boys from prairie towns.

I've grown bolder since you left.
I cut off my hair when it wouldn't curl.

28

I shoot squirrels in my dressing-gown, leaving the bodies
for the other squirrels to find, as warning or wish.

I'll cross the territory, soon as you send word.

*In small towns such as these*
*        where I, too, was born,*
*each says yes to what she is supposed to*
*        and no to what she is*
*supposed to refuse.*

*What dark thing changed the ordinary*
*        doings of ordinary citizens*
*into messages?*

*Life as a rural queer still isn't easy.*

*Shame turning strangers into relations.*

# Rearview

That harvest brought a good yield.
I was still in skirts,
she a *marm,* the youngest
spinster schoolteacher.
I wanted to learn mapmaking
& husbandry.

I built a chair for her
chaste. She flat-footed
into the kitchen
munching on sweets.

Only two
funerals since summer,
grandparents reaching their time.
I snuck into her barn,
wet my lips
in the fresh milk
of her best cow.
A crust of ice broke
on my tongue. Her fingers
found my neck
beneath a blue knit scarf.
I wanted to plant an orchard
for her, be more
than a hired hand.

She handed me
a late-born midnight

lamb to warm beneath
my coat as her mother
took ill. Up in the sky,
just before all went black,
flakes fell like stars
in the candlelight.
She read me so well.

At the thaw, she wore
a lighter color, a new hat.
I collected suspenders & jackets.
She showed me how to sew a seam,
foreshorten. Our island,
behind a haystack,
where we shared scars.

She led me to the library,
her new employ.
Secret books became mirrors.
Midnight wound her way
between our legs,
& the weather turned.
I slept in her barn
as her family died,
one by one. They hated us
& her face watered my lap.

Every strand of the cornsilk
tresses, untamed on my head
she mourned.

I rode to Menahga
for the bands & lace.
She buried her nose
in my neck, arms woven
around my thickening waist.

She didn't know
how regular this leaving
was already.
I wanted to give her
a world, hold a lozenge
up to the light,
watch her smile shine.

I never trusted my body
not to betray us.

*What else could Frank reply*

*to every woman with a request in their eyes?*


*Sex is the only time*

*I belong in my body.*



*slick*          *kissing tree*

*unlace me*

## Ars Erotica

Plunge beneath my skirt
and reach til you touch my beard.
Merely feel with your fingers
and I am happy.

Then—gently—turn over upon me.
The twirl of your tongue—
sweet electric fire, caged breath.
Lick my hip bones all over.

My female form—
salted breasts, split fruit,
slope, and sag of bone—
blood, flesh, flame.

I fill a chamber of dew
for you—oyster flower,
purple thrush,
tufted nest.

And I lay my head in your lap,
breathless until dawn.

# Helpmate III

For a woman, walking alone ain't easy.
Boys in this city throw dead cats

through our window. Tramps & incendiaries
haunt the doorstep & slit throats in the barn.

Lonely urge, poor man made.
Beside the lake with clear water, we wed.

Petals arranged & benches overturned.
A clerk & preacher; neither suspected.

We honey-mooned on horseback,
on the road to Milwaukee.

I slid my hand above her garters,
unlocked the twist of her thighs.

## UNSTONED

I wouldn't let them touch me—
the gals I knew before.

They rucked up skirts & wound
their ankles round my waist.

I put my hands inside their thighs
& pressed until the pleasure came.

A Detroit whore tried to undress me;
her dirty nails marked half

circles into my shoulder. I sunk
my reddened lips into her tired

bosom as my fingers arranged ministrations.
A widow lost her husband young

& liked my smooth, small hands.
She wanted to play at marriage bed

& pinned my hair beneath a hat.
I was barely fifteen. She trimmed a nail,

crafted a mustache, & showed me how
to sink inside, to make myself moan along.

I've always walked rough, tamed the fields
with Pa, & rode astride even in skirts.

You came along like a cat, flicking your tail
beneath blooming trees, cocking a chin, & whispering

close. Fabric roughens my thighs, but standing
& smoking, drinking & spitting, I pass.

Towns see what they want—no horse
too thin these days, no woman unlucky

enough. We move around counties,
explorers forging new states. I learn to shoot

or steal our food those times I'm lying around
loose. But inside, far away, you put me in a bonnet,

lift my petticoats on your knees, & show me
how to be strong. Our flowers never

wilt, our bells ring long, & only you
know what my mother called me.

*the leaves forced by wind off the tree*

       *illness*
       *sleeplessness*
       *irritable despair*

*her lips*               *my wife*

*her footsteps in the kitchen*

*survive but do not move*

       *I am not giving voice to the voiceless*
       *I am trying to figure out how to be*
       *imprisoned (pleasantly) in desire.*

# CALL & RESPONSE

<u>The Townsfolk</u>

In case of emergency, we build our fences high,
our barns sturdy, our women of iron. Our boys
swim naked in the crick, and train tracks skirt
our town, carrying trouble away. Dissent,
liquor, and impurity must be chased down. Worry
settles like dust in the lines of grandmothers'
faces. These are troubled times, the ice house
knowing naught of ice.

<u>Gertrude</u>

I tried to leave a dozen times,
but smoke fills the stove.
Anna puts her mouth
on some other lady's hip
and I am bereft. I cling to a pillow
in her absence, my hand splayed across
my empty womb.

## The Author

*Two birds sit on a line.*
*I watch through my window;*
*flapping wings, cawing.*
*Sometimes, in profile, they look*
*like one large bird. Sometimes*
*they are a different species altogether.*
*Women are like this, when we live*
*side by side, years stretched between*
*us like laundry. Top and bottom,*
*butch and femme, lover and beloved.*
*Nothing is static. Everything shared.*

*Each contains both birds.*

*All things are feral.*
*Tame: a myth. Still, our wives want us*
*on a leash and leathered.*

## The Telegrapher

Eighty-eight is code for love and kisses.

Ladies send notes for gingham, plaid, flannel.
Husbands out West wire for cash, and gals
sell their hair and jewels. A visiting opera
singer receives notices from New York City;
urgent obituaries funnel through my fingers.
Dots and dashes intertwine on paper for lovers
faraway. A slim-faced tomboy in church dress
weeps on the bench outside. She pays me
with a chicken. Her husband is in jail, and no
lawyer will arrive. Dismay hollows her eyes.

I chart the passage of love and time.

Anna

There are years when nothing happens.

We go on collecting hat pins, dusting stairs.

I've started to wear my ma's clothes.

Mine have all been burned.

I do not usually look so like a girl.

Dogs chew at the hem of such skirts, prairie colored and thick.

So much of my skin is shielded, but it is no remedy.

I cannot put myself right concerning this impulse for you.

At church they tell me Nature is all God's power.

I just go for the hymns.

The Newspaperman

After the sentence was passed, the smaller woman,
much bereaved, clung to the larger woman's suspenders.
I thought of my own wife, May, how she repeats this action
each morning, stuffing pencil and paper scraps into my pocket,
guessing the time I'll be home for dinner by the weather
and gossip in the air.

Theft alone isn't news. There is always a story beneath the story.

## The Author

*My fiancée and I crossed the border,*
*met with a minister*
*who asked what we would do about*
*money and sex. Fighting about both*
*was in our future, but then,*
*solace reigned. We clutched hands,*
*cut eyes, and our smiles were fluorescent.*

*Some days I want to roam. I imagine*
*the peaceful solitude of wind across*
*a prairie. But left behind, imagining*
*her voice saying someone else's name,*
*I know that wrath comes first, then lack.*

*Some mistakes are consciously made.*
*Others are inevitable; inchoate unions*
*built on absence and fear.*

The Harlot

Frank never stays long,
and never sits
on the bed.
I bend over my dressing table
and watch his eyes
in the mirror. China hands
hug my hips. Teeth
leave their imprint
on my shoulder. Sweat leaks
through my slip, bunched up
at the waist. Even when unruly,
my breasts are hushed doves
beneath his fingers. Rude gent,
yet tender as one who knows
the pain of misplacement.

## The Cellmate

In life outside, I tended roses.
It was my duty to outshine
the cleverness of rabbits
bent on destruction. Inside,
we are the ones subject to treatments.
Our thorns trimmed, vices
corralled. My husband loved
two things: whiskey and
uprooting roses. I am vigilant
when it comes to weeds.
When I used the sheep shears
to trim back thistles, I was
inventive. When I used them
to split open my husband's throat:
a mortal sin. This new cellmate
is a thief. They say she's someone's
husband. I mistrust her glances.
I know what a husband can steal.

## The Preacher

Apostle Paul said it is better
to marry than to be aflame
with passion. He saw the difference
between such states.

## The Author

*Women are words to me now.*
*I dress them like paper dolls,*
*press their thin faces together*
*in a kiss. My own divorce is*
*fresh-faced as Anna out*
*riding her mare in the snow.*

*Marriage confounds me.*
*I am trying to erect a shelter*
*in which to cache my nerves.*
*I am trying to tell you a story*
*of my life: you split the apple*
*with a knife, held one half up*
*to my lips. The spilled juice*
*stained our bed. Whose hand?*
*Whose lips? Whose dress?*
*My body betrays my endeavors.*

# True North

A girlfriend is a safety net, a surefire prayer
on Sundays, a fatback meal on the table,

a mender & star shooter, something to ride
home about. Midsummer eve I bathed in the river,

broad hips floating & chafed thighs aching
for her phantom fingers.

Her eyes, sapphire in the dark,
called up stray hand, lost key, howling dog.

Her skin sparked, her kiss turned;
all our kin watched & applauded.

She appears in such dreams more often these days,
as the fires threaten our haunts,

& the road remains winding & subtle.
I blew every seed askew wishing

for safe passage, light water, & sure-shot game.
I wish on thistle, on loon's call & spider's

webbed snare. I sleep beneath a quilt she made—
a seafarer's north star, from my torn britches

& her faded petticoat. Long ago in youth,
I reached in & plucked her from myself

& put her in my dreams. Don't trouble my course;
all waters & lovers return to their source.

*The moments in the day or night*
*when you think to yourself:*
*this is adulthood,*
*this is your life.*


*Still I remember*
*when you penetrated my uneasiness*
*plagued with soft fears and tender hostilities.*

*We have sufficiently graduated our advances.*


*overcoming inertia (body in motion)*

# CUPID'S ITCH

When the stench of other women
grows too thick on your neck,
I take to the skies, sketching
birds of every variety.
I don't believe the books—
no one mates for life;
not quite.

You came home with Cupid's Itch.
I packed my bag, walked to town for potatoes,
and went on with the stew.

The rash and silence spread as you filled in your shirt,
every breadcrumb free or stolen.
We cut eyes across the table, fuming
and squirrelly. I washed the chalk off the wall,
my countdown of absence and competing suitors.

I live as a wife, but I am not a wife.
I wound a golden strand of grass around
your finger and we wed one night
in the meadow, breasts thick and still.
The fires of home blazing,
my petticoat awash by the river.

I envy everyone else who lays a finger—
the barber, cutting your hair;
the tailor whose trim tends too close.

Recall the night my blade nicked
your ears, my voice assuring that
the new face in the glass was yours.

Snow threatens these hills,
and I pray for drifts so high
we think we're buried—

When you offer escape,
I cannot resist—
I'd travel anywhere beyond the reach
of all the whispering graves—
too shallow, too soon.

Every few years, we meet the woman
who calls you by a name I've never known.
Letters follow, every word a fiction. You speak
of your wife to others, and of reform.

She talks of travel, but the return address
remains static. No seaside or sunshine
to warm a widow's heart.

Envy curls alongside her neat rows of letters,
so prim and volatile.

Don't you think I have noticed
how you never write my name?

# GOOD HOUSEKEEPING

Townsfolk frown that we have no kin, no kids.
Old women pass me tips at the mercantile,
ways to place our bodies in the dark, potions

to swallow, and meals that will prepare my womb.
There are entire chapters of my housekeeping books
that will never apply. I fold their pages back, hide

my wishes inside corners I've used to smash bugs.
Imagine—one night, you poured a tonic over me;
a daughter born the next day; one more garden to uproot.

## EQUATIONS

A sapphire necklace to adorn my neck,
a handful of coins and bills.
I helped you stoke the fire.

They pull off your pants in the jail.
My voice catches, arms outstretched.

I clasp your soiled knuckles and
our mouths' proximity frightens the sheriff.
No more holding hands; no breathing close.

I wanted to go far away into the green
pine dust to float on light with you.
Now I know the consequences—two take away one.

I'll find a way. I'll never flee.

Stretched out in the sun,
my mouth finding every tattoo
that makes a painted desert,
tracing tributaries of stretchmarks,
my tongue charting the way a river
hugs the earth, the way your freckles,
dimples, scars mark the landmass
of your body.

Clit and tongue, fist, cunt, fuck, unfurl, forget
the way even your best friend curls her lip
when you talk about sucking strap-on cock,
banish memories of men sure they know
what you must really need.

Shadows, swells, the trembling
prairie between your thighs,
I explore everything, your perfect
imperfect flesh, alcove for my hand,
the Central Lowland beneath
your naval, the meandering scars
down your spine, shimmering
like salt flats. Friction and feathers,

sandpaper and silk, hair like a bridal
veil fall, the water that mists
over the rocks like gauze, never
quite reaching the pool below. Your
hair glows, spread off the edge of our
bed. It is so simple, me on my knees,

*so complicated, ankles on my shoulders—*
*there's nothing we can't do—*
*so holy the way you see me, and I see you.*

## Call Me by My Other Name

Sheriff's gun butt at my back,
my resistance to disrobe in the jail.
Coins scatter at my feet, enough
to buy us flour, sugar, meat for months.

My hands stretch behind me,
the pins of my bindings break.
Now he has found my holster,
emptied me of any defense.

Buttons torn, trousers loosened,
his fist hard on my teeth, eyes
suspicious and cold. Just as his hand
goes to his belt, the deputy turning

his head to the window, you burst in
shouting my other name.
They say we never will return home.
In school, we studied plagues in Egypt

and fashions in Europe. Some children
pulled the legs off every bug.
You dreamed of lace petticoats, crinolines,
garments requiring help to unbutton.

I am old enough now to mistress myself.
But what will you do without my facility
for heavy loads and numbers?

# Gertrude Visits the Jailhouse

In the dark room,

we sit facing each other,

moonlight thick as milk

on a rough wooden table.

My hands are quiet and smooth

on her hands, those hewn

from straw grip and bridle.

This absence is sharper

than the sins I made up.

Love: a woolen garment

too frayed to darn.

We learn to live with those spaces

the cold always finds.

Voices mix and rise—

other prisoners

saying goodbye;

a psalm of whispers.

*The way my tongue can't stop*
*worrying        the sore tooth*

*I can't stop imagining myself*
*into the 19<sup>th</sup> century*

*or mourning the ease I've felt with you my whole life*

*Do I have the temerity to be a boy?*
*Or what it takes to withstand betrayal?*

# Distance Cuts No Figure

I get little sleep
& what there is of it is troubled.

Every prisoner wants to know
how I made it happen &
what kind of damage fifteen years
of horse glue makes on a gal's
fair features.

*Ten cents for a mustache,*
*eighty buys a full beard.*

I've been in trousers
since I was ten.

Here, my legs are bare
as Gertie's plucked chickens.
Prison dress wilts around me.

Guards menace us ceaselessly.
There are twenty women
in my one cell. We huddle,
clench & steel.

It takes about a week
for new contusions
to fade into the blur
of habitual bruises.

I have three years.
Days lose themselves,
ghosting one into the next.

I dream of fields filled with women
I've been longing for my whole life.

## Jailbird's Song

I wanted to marry an absence; Gertrude is flesh,
bone, bruise. An anchor, though I outlast the need to moor.
I'll always be an outlaw, & sometimes I have no grief, only
the sound of my many names, shouted to the wind.


I write my best letters in bed, sign each with an alias, ink
staining the sheets, conversation fluid, & the next in a line
of brunettes at my pillow.


What I love: thrown-back throats,
eyes squeezed shut, so I become a hankering between their knees.
*Seamus, Gil, Robert & Joe*—the names women scream to the night.
Only my heart won't stop whispering *oh Frank, oh Anna*. Bite my ear,
beg me for all the jewels in the world, weeping into your apron.


You are the headline's yawn, the hollow mouths of my cellmates,
the chafe of shackles & tight grip of skin, ring, wallet.
I never told you of the four men it took to hold me still, the raw
eggs they slipped down my throat, nor what else followed.
Though I have the sharpest hand on a muzzle—of a horse or a gun—
prison doctors found a way around my nature.


First I dreamt of felted soap, empty cradles, advent chocolates, & childhood
prayers. The vacant sound of hooves. One night, I traded my saddle
for whiskey & a blanket. The swell of blood in my jaw & missing
buttons will bring me home quicker than salted meat or tarnished gold.

*The first flame-haired lady*
*who approached my cage of desire*
*recoiled:*        *"You're not a boy."*

*Brisk and early, I molded my form*
       *for her.*

*After all these years of losing,*
*it was finding her in another woman's*
*bed that finally crushed me.*

       *No matter how I bind*
          *my body*
*will be wrong.*

*I wed the Wasatch mountains*
*when my wife left again;*
*a year later, we were legalized.*

*Ice slowed my severe blood,*
*unbridled me.*

*In a whiskey town*
*I forgot how it felt*
*to be requited.*

*Crude tools for being human.*
*But I'm no longer scared of solitude.*

# Pictures of Women with Men They Did Not Marry

Winter hit town hard that year.
Strong men were found weeping.

Charlie had a barnful of dynamite
from the boarded-up mine.

He had criminal ears, thick and
sticking out—they tickled

my chin when he suckled my buttons.
It was the season of crinkled ribbon,

limp limbs, and tiny coffins, the bare feet
blowing in the wind of the folks hanged from a tree.

He held my hand behind the church,
shared his curious superstitions.

Years later he dressed his wife like a deer
and blew up their barn:

*Here I go and the Lord go with me.*

*

The year of flooding and one sister gone,
Donald held me close.

He picked water weeds along the shore,
fed goslings from his hand.

He took me on the river in a boat,
though the banks boiled over.

*The rooster crows where the corpse lies.*

Somewhere out West he settled, my sister Sarah
consenting to what I could not.

She writes that dust follows them everywhere,
clings like a persistent child to her skirts.

*

The dead girl's here again.
She visits each summer,

making sandcastles at the lakeshore,
leading boys to my bed.

When I'm in the bath, I hear her coughing.
In the glass, as I wash my face,

I think she has my eyes. At the asylum they say
this comes with the weather—

patients deranged on the subject of religion,
disposed to injure others.

Bradley proved the trouble with young people
in springtime—

drug taking, arson, lovelorn suicide.
He said I drove him to do it.

You see, I could have won a man
had I the desire, but your beard tickles me,

your hands are soft beneath my shirt.
No, my female husband does not speak of my sisters,

nor the symphony of smashing and shooting,
the music of breaking glass we left behind.

*Noticed darkness at 5:08pm. -2 degrees.*
　　　　*Now reading by candlelight.*

　　*Ten years, more or less,*
　　*since my face tasted fire.*

*The pain in my eyes, squinting to fix a loose hem*
*even by the table lamp's glow.*

*Riding my horse on the farm,*
*I close my eyes and I could be*
*Anna in empty fields,*

　　　*the ubiquitous tug*
　　*at the undergarments.*

　*My dirt-stained hands,*

　　*tangled hair;*

*I have been on my knees at the keyhole*

*but the thought of thighs and cheeks*
　　*kissed by muslin does after all make me swoon.*

## ANNA SUCCUMBS TO DIPHTHERIA

How red your face—
fever our excuse for isolation, a homestead

far from town, snuggling up
and dressing down. Forming figures uncanny.

Familiar; I recognize this wheezing.
Plump your pillows; full eiderdown

delays breath's flight. Let the doctor
not examine too close, tighten your shirt,

voice low, faint. You seem a boy
with honest face and unrough hands.

I pray for your throat—color of fresh milk.
My delicate lips' hollow—may he not

carve you out. Guard your chest;
I'll look away when the silver shows,

straighten my bonnet and play dutiful
wife. Worry not for work;

I'll sell my gilded hat pin,
blue gloves, and wedding band.

But, my beau, shall we be discovered—
we must take to the train again. A move

to a Minnesota town with a dreamy name—
St. Cloud, a place above this mean existence.


Or we could ranch out West—where mountains
reach eagles and there's space and lions yet. Say your lungs


are swollen, chest tumescent. Speak the spell
I told to you, sweat-stained, sheets bloody;


delay the laudanum.
I will not cling to your coffin just yet.

# GOSSIP

Her hair is a tattered thundercloud
where once her lambskin brow
launched men from trains.

They still tell stories of the widow,
always looking the other way,
watching for that telltale dust
coming up off the road, the signal
that her husband's riding home.

Looking from the front porch
of her homestead far from town
was one thing—the doctor
told the men in the saloon
of her far-off eyes—

but now that Mrs. Blunt lives in town,
she should know she's alone,
that her husband ain't never comin' home.

Still she waits for a soft-featured man to return,
dressed in black cheviot suits,
kangaroo calf shoes, her gaze recalling
how his fingertips kissed hers.

# Helpmate IV

She has a taste for the bejeweled.
I rob the store & scoot,

mustache slipping with sweat. My skirts—
discovered. Gertie weeps for half an hour.

She falls upon my neck in the jail.
The papers don't call it love:

*Wouldn't use that word for anything a pair of girls could do.*

## Pastoral

Desperate men do not make patient women.

This town, these years, always living on the edge of something.

Disease, drought, revival, recession.

The woods are musky, dark, but give way softly to water.

Fish and stags float when shot dead.

One year there was no rain; the next, rivers overflowed.

Not a hell mouth or hydrophobic, but even the air here is tainted.

The ice never quite crusts over, babies are left untended, crops go missing.

My wife won't quit visiting whores.

Recall the rhyme we sang in school:

*For every evil under the sun,*
*There is a remedy, or there is none.*
*If there be one, try and find it;*
*If there be none, never mind it.*

Our hands in a circle clapped for every word;
we thought we'd smash sin like a bug.

It hid inside us, coiled, knowing someday we'd stray.

But who's to say which sin is ours?
Each time I read your letters, I see things differently.

Why shouldn't scripture be the same?

Grass caught in our teeth as we laughed, rolling down hills like barrels,
the curves of each mound forgiving but spoken for.

There is no remedy for us—

*I can't say it's never lonely in Queer America.*

*And the punishments for visibility are real and terrible.*

*But we have always been everywhere.*

*Bearing the burden and responsibility of scarcity,*

*we have long been so beautiful in each other's gaze.*


*I still thrill at your touch; I still feel the shock*

*of fear when your fingers meet mine in public.*

*If we are alone, it is the loneliness of crowds.*

## DEATH TRIP

If anyone had asked,
Anna would have said death
was like plowing the fields
on a hot day. That fever—
soaking her soul into the bed linens.
The gray rag Gertrude dragged
across her forehead—just like any cloth
she used to wipe her brow, then tucked
back under the straw hat as she sat atop the nag.

& sure enough, turning her head back,
suddenly, to the task at hand, that hiccough
of the plow hitting a rock whose head
just barely peeked out of the ground,
the rest spreading out, buried deep,
taking the whole day to clear.
That's what the journey resembled
but without the sun ever sinking down,
with none of Gertie's lemonade,
served in a dusty mug.

Anna sank her hands right into the dirt,
didn't bother with a shovel this time,
sure to clear every bit of that stone to discover
what had been withheld these long years.

They'd argued much about the outfit
she should don to meet the Almighty. Gertrude

of one strong opinion, as always. Disagreeing;
resolute about the dress.

Yet what a surprise it was to learn clothes didn't matter,
that God more than anyone knew what name to call her.

# CALL ME BY MY OTHER NAME

## Notes

I was inspired to write this collection of poems after reading a newspaper clipping from Michael Lesy's book *Wisconsin Death Trip*, a piece from the *Badger State Banner*, 1894, which is printed in the beginning of this book.

I have attempted to make the book historically accurate according to known events, but the characters as they exist on these pages are fictionalized. I've gained much inspiration from my research, including works by other authors, as specified below.

"Make You Feel My Love" takes its title from the Bob Dylan song.

"Ars Erotica" was inspired by Whitman.

"Jailbird's Song" takes its initial phrase from a poem by Thomas James.

"Pictures of Women with Men They Did Not Marry" takes its title and paraphrases some lines from an unpublished work by JaNeill Weseloh.

## Acknowledgments

Grateful acknowledgment is made to the editors of the following publications in which these poems first appeared.

*Bloom*: The One with Violets in Her Lap
*Drunken Boat*: Make You Feel My Love
*Ink Node*: Helpmate & So Long as Men-Folk Stay Away
*Western Humanities Review*: Unlike Lesser Gods
                                          & I Need No Disguises to Woo

The poems "Pastoral" and "Call & Response" also appeared in the anthology *When We Become Weavers: Queer Female Poets on the Midwestern Experience* (Squares & Rebels Press 2012, ed. Kate Lynn Hibbard). "The One with Violets in Her Lap" and "Make You Feel My Love" also appeared in the chapbook *Bad Wife Spankings* (Gertrude Press 2010).

This book was the labor of a decade, and I have many people to thank for their help along the path. Special thanks to Mark Wunderlich, for first loaning me *Wisconsin Death Trip* and suggesting it as a writing exercise I never could put down. Thank you to the friends, colleagues, and teachers who helped in the writing of this book: Anna Morrison, Erin Belieu, Andrew Epstein, David Kirby, Eric Walker, Pete Kunze, Stephen S. Mills, Rebecca Lehman, Rebecca Hazelton, the Blue Door Poets, Katharine Coles, Paisley Rekdal, Jacqueline Osherow, C.A. Schaefer, Erin Rogers, Meg Day, Barbara Duffey, Chandler Klang Smith, Shira Dentz, Tasha Matsumoto, Jessica Rae Bergamino, Laura Passin, Katharine Donelson, and Catie Crabtree for your advice and friendship.

Thank you to April Ossman, Mark Doty, Matthew Zapruder, and D. Gilson who provided necessary and heartfelt feedback.

Thank you to everyone who read my first book and kept asking what I was writing next.

For the incredible cover art, my thanks to fellow Iowan Sharon Gochenour, who created custom artwork even better than I could have imagined.

My continual thanks to Bryan Borland, Seth Pennington, and everyone at Sibling Rivalry Press for believing in my work and welcoming me into the family.

All my gratitude to my family who have always loved me & supported me unconditionally. I know just how lucky I am for that.

## About the Poet

Valerie Wetlaufer is a teacher, editor, and poet. She holds a BA in French and an MA in Teaching from Bennington College, an MFA in Poetry from the Florida State University, and a PhD in Literature & Creative Writing from the University of Utah, where she was a Vice Presidential Fellow. Her first book, *Mysterious Acts by My People* (Sibling Rivalry Press, 2014) won the Lambda Literary Award for Lesbian Poetry. She lives in Cedar Rapids, Iowa.

## About the Cover Artist

Sharon J. Gochenour is an explorer of many places and many media and concerned with light in all of them. She has researched daylighting and architecture in Boston, Tokyo, and Lausanne; she has investigated light with ink and paint in Iowa, Spain, France, and a few other locales.

## About the Press

Sibling Rivalry Press is an independent press based in Little Rock, Arkansas. Its mission is to publish work that disturbs and enraptures. This book was published in part due to the support of the Sibling Rivalry Press Foundation, a non-profit private foundation dedicated to assisting small presses and small press authors.